ESL
READING
AND SPELLING

Games, Puzzles, and Inventive Exercises

by Imogene Forte
and Mary Ann Pangle

Incentive Publications, Inc.
Nashville, Tennessee

Illustrated by Marta Drayton
Cover by Marta Drayton
Edited by Jean K. Signor

ISBN 0-86530-488-2

PRINTED IN THE UNITED STATES OF AMERICA
www.incentivepublications.com

Table of Contents

Reading and Spelling

HOW TO USE THIS BOOK

Learning is the focal point of the activities included in <u>ESL Reading and Spelling Games, Puzzles, and Inventive Exercises</u> and the content-based nature of the exercises ensures that students are learning more than English. This book will be a valuable tool for all teachers who work with students learning English as a second language (ESL); the books in this series will be helpful for or with students needing additional reinforcement with acquisition of basic language skills.

Each activity is skills-based to develop language concepts, and understandings connected to a specific skill. Additionally, the exercises in this book offer opportunity for learning, practicing, and mastery of a variety of essential language based skills. Each exercise includes a list of materials, preparation directions, and player directions. Many exercises have accompanying reproducible activity sheets for immediate classroom skill and/or concept reinforcement. A reading and spelling skills matrix, a suggested bibliography for additional references, and an answer key are also provided. These tools are designed to help teachers plan their lessons and track the achievement of their students. Each lesson is designed for use by ESL students at widely varying age and grade levels.

Students need to use learned material, and practice plays an essential role in the mastery and retention of any skill or concept. In addition to individual worksheets, many exercises provide activities that promote cooperative learning and peer tutoring. Cooperative learning activities are essential in an ESL classroom as they enable students to work collaboratively to verbalize, refine, and process newly acquired knowledge and skills. The themes of high-interest on which these activities are based will further encourage student interaction and communication.

This book was written with an eye on the Cognitive Academic Language Learning Approach (CALLA). Accordingly, the exercises encourage the four major conditions of this teaching method: first, to foster a learning environment of high expectations; secondly, to create opportunities to integrate language development with content-based instruction; thirdly, to provide support for teachers in the classroom; and finally, to demonstrate assessment options that empower teachers to plan effective lessons for their students.

The games, puzzles, and exercises within <u>ESL Reading and Spelling Games, Puzzles, and Inventive Exercises</u> will help teachers make the most effective use of their time in helping their ESL students to learn essential reading and spelling skills, improve their use of the English language, and acquire problem-solving skills and concepts important to student success.

Reading and Spelling Skills Matrix

	Alphabetical Order	Comprehension	Punctuate Sentences Correctly	Spelling & Writing Practice	Nouns	Consonants and Syllables	Follow Written Directions	Rhyming & New Words	Encyclopedia Use	Vowels	Abbreviations	Speaking
Content Focus: Reading												
Animal Alphabet	+	+										
Snowflake Fun	+											
Sentence Sense			+	+								
Needy Nouns		+		+	+			+				
Noble Nouns		+			+							
Letter Lingo	+						+	+				
Appropriate Abbreviations							+	+			+	
Singular vs. Plural		+						+				
Encyclopedia Explorers		+		+					+			
Vowel Volcano				+						+		
The Lost Balloon		+	+	+			+	+		+		
Blend Bonanza					+	+						
Hidden Pictures							+	+				
Direction Detective		+		+			+					
The Snowman		+		+		+						
Syllable Spies				+	+	+						
Secret Code	+											
Content Focus: Spelling												
Tic Tac Toe				+				+				+
Blast Off				+				+				+
Spelling Checkers				+				+				+
Drive and Spell				+				+				+
Correct Colors				+				+				+
Play Ball				+				+				+

ESL Reading and Spelling
Games, Puzzles, and Inventive Exercises

ESL Reading and Spelling Games, Puzzles, and Inventive Exercises

Animal Alphabet

Purpose:

> **Reading** - Alphabetical Order

Materials:

> Copy of Alphabet Cards
>
> Scissors
>
> Pencils
>
> Crayons

Number of Players:

> One, or the entire class

Preparation Directions:

> 1. Give each player a copy of the game cards.
>
> 2. Each player cuts out a copy of the game cards.

Player Directions:

> 1. The players cut out Alphabet Cards.
>
> 2. The players identify the animal pictured on each card.
>
> 3. Then the players draw and color a picture the animal name that is written on the card, or the players write the name of the animal pictured on the card.
>
> 4. The players arrange the cards in alphabetical order on their desks.

Giraffe

Octopus

Cat

Iguana

Nightingale

Jellyfish

Yak

11

Lion

Bear

Zebra

Kangaroo

Elephant

Vulture

Snowflake Fun

Purpose:

Reading - Alphabet

Materials:

Copy of Snowflake Fun Maze

Follow-up activity

Pencils

Crayons

Number of Players:

One, or the entire class

Preparation Directions:

1. Give each player a copy of the maze.

2. Give each player a copy of the follow-up activity.

3. Provide pencils and crayons

Player Directions:

1. The player or players follow the directions on the maze.

2. After completing the maze, the player or players follow the directions on the follow-up activity.

Snowflake Fun

Make your way through the snowstorm.

START HERE

YOU MADE IT!

*ESL Reading and Spelling
Games, Puzzles, and Inventive Exercises*

Begin with the letter Z and go backwards to the letter A to complete the picture.

*ESL Reading and Spelling
Games, Puzzles, and Inventive Exercises*

Sentence Sense

Purpose:

Reading - Sentence Structure

Materials:

Sentence Sense game board for each student

Game markers

Small plastic cube

Number of Players:

Two or three players

Preparation Directions:

1. Write the numbers 1 and 2 on the side of the game cube.

2. Provide a copy of the Sentence Sense game board for each set of students.

3. Provide each player with a game marker.

Player Directions:

1. The first player rolls the die and moves the correct number of spaces.

2. If the space is marked (. ! or ?), the player must make up a sentence that ends with that punctuation mark.

3. If the player does not supply a correct sentence, he or she moves back one space.

4. The game continues until one player reaches "Finish" to win the game.

Sentence Sense Game Board

*ESL Reading and Spelling
Games, Puzzles, and Inventive Exercises*

Needy Nouns

Purpose:

> **Reading** - Proper Nouns

Materials:

> Copy of the game
> Pencils
> Crayons

Number of Players:

> An entire class or small groups

Preparation Directions:

> 1. Give each student a copy of the game.
> 2. Have a class discussion to review proper nouns.

Player Directions:

> 1. The students are to write a proper noun for each item on the shelves.
> 2. The proper nouns can be brand names or students can create their own proper nouns.
> 3. After the activity is completed, students may color the pictures.
> 4. Sharing the activities will build vocabulary.

Noble Nouns

Purpose:

Reading - Common and Proper Nouns

Materials:

Copy of game cards

Scissors

Number of Players:

Two

Preparation Directions:

1. Give each group of players a copy of the game cards.

2. Each player cuts out a copy of the game cards.

Player Directions:

1. The game cards are shuffled and placed face down.

2. The first player draws a card and reads it.

3. The first player must say a proper noun for the common noun that is written on the card.

4. If the answer is correct, the player receives one point.

5. The game continues until all of the cards are used.

6. The player who receives the most points wins the game.

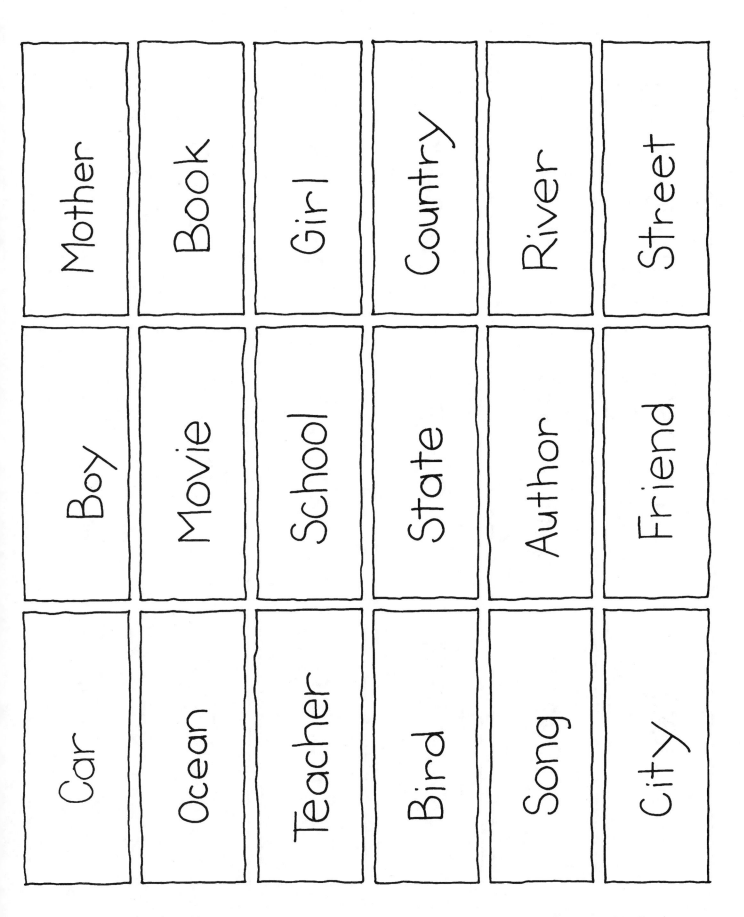

Mother	Book	Girl	Country	River	Street
Boy	Movie	School	State	Author	Friend
Car	Ocean	Teacher	Bird	Song	City

ESL Reading and Spelling
Games, Puzzles, and Inventive Exercises

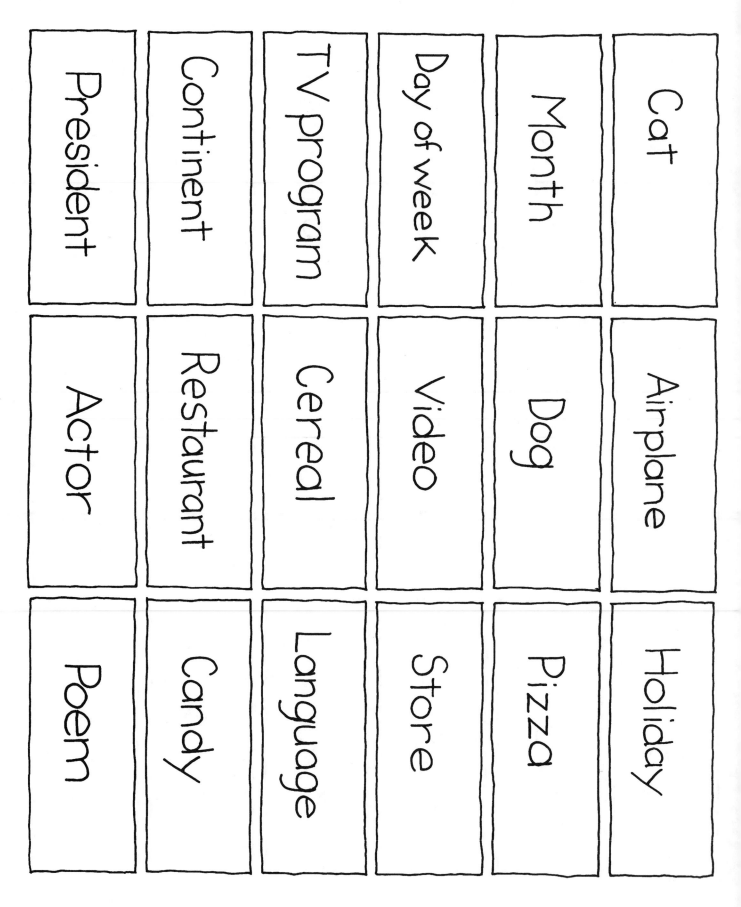

President	Continent	TV program	Day of week	Month	Cat
Actor	Restaurant	Cereal	Video	Dog	Airplane
Poem	Candy	Language	Store	Pizza	Holiday

Letter Lingo

Purpose:

Reading - Phonics

Materials:

Copy of the activity

Pencils

Crayons

Number of Players:

One

Preparation Directions:

1. Give each player a copy of the activity.

2. Provide pencils and crayons.

Player Directions:

1. The player looks at each picture and writes the letter of its beginning sound. This will spell a word.

2. In the box, the player illustrates each word.

ESL Reading and Spelling
Games, Puzzles, and Inventive Exercises

Letter Lingo Activity

1. Write the letter for each picture.
2. Then illustrate each new word.

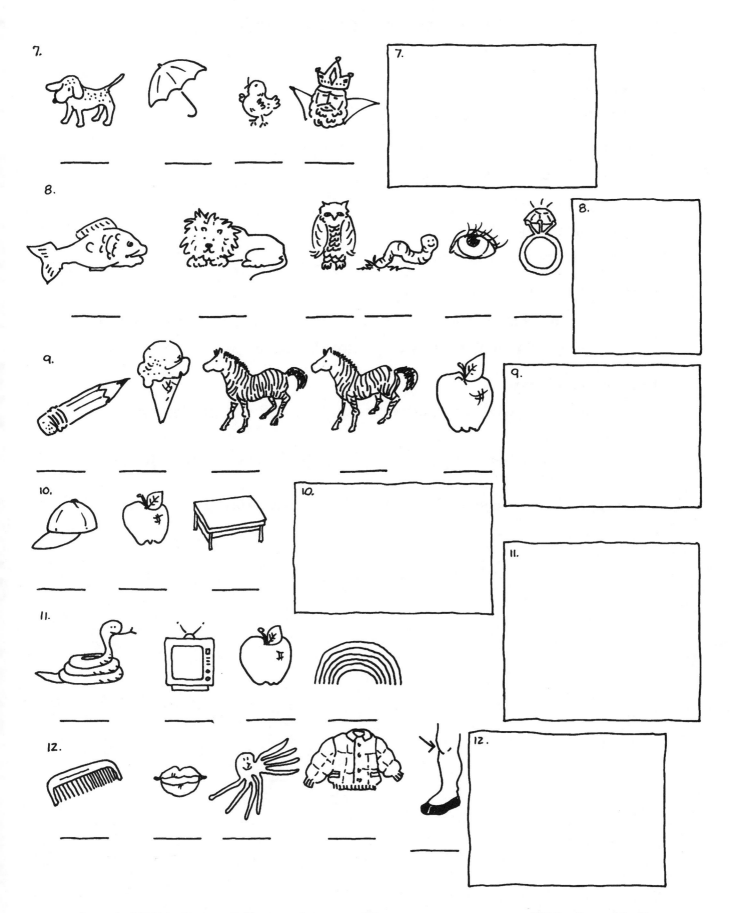

7. _____

8. _____

9. _____

10. _____

11. _____

12. _____

Appropriate Abbreviations

Purpose:

Reading - Vocabulary

Materials:

Copy of the crossword puzzle

Pencils

Number of Players:

One, two, or the entire class

Preparation Directions:

1. Give each player a copy of the crossword puzzle and provide pencils.

2. Review abbreviations with the entire class or in small groups.

Player Directions:

1. The players will enjoy working in small cooperative groups for this activity.

2. The players read the directions and write the abbreviations for the words in the correct spaces.

3. Provide time to share the answers to the crossword puzzle.

Appropriate Abbreviations Crossword Puzzle

Directions: For each word or phrase below, write the correct abbreviation.

ACROSS

1. Monday
4. street
5. Ounce
7. minute
9. Tennessee
10. Afternoon
13. Reverend
14. doctor
16. dozen
19. October
21. President
24. Spelling
25. Sunday
29. April
30. Doctor of Medicine
31. Wednesday
33. March

DOWN

1. Mister
2. November
3. Railroad
4. Saturday
6. Vice President
7. Mathematics
8. number
11. August
12. Road
15. September
17. all right
18. mile
20. Tuesday
21. pint
22. Senior
23. North
26. Thursday
27. January
28. February
30. married woman
32. feet
33. Mile

*ESL Reading and Spelling
Games, Puzzles, and Inventive Exercises*

Singular vs. Plural

Purpose:

Reading - Vocabulary

Materials:

Copy of game board
Copy of game cards
Scissors
Markers

Number of Players:

Two or four

Preparation Directions:

1. Give the players a copy of the game board and game cards.

2. Provide scissors and markers for the students.

3. Review plurals as an entire class.

Player Directions:

1. The players cut out the game cards and place them face down.

2. The players place the markers on "Start" on the game board.

3. The first player draws a card and pronounces the word that is written on it.

4. If the word is singular, the player spells the plural of it.

5. If the word is plural, the player spells the singular of it.

6. If the player is correct, he or she moves one space.

7. The game continues until one player reaches "Finish" and wins the game.

Singular vs. Plural Game Board

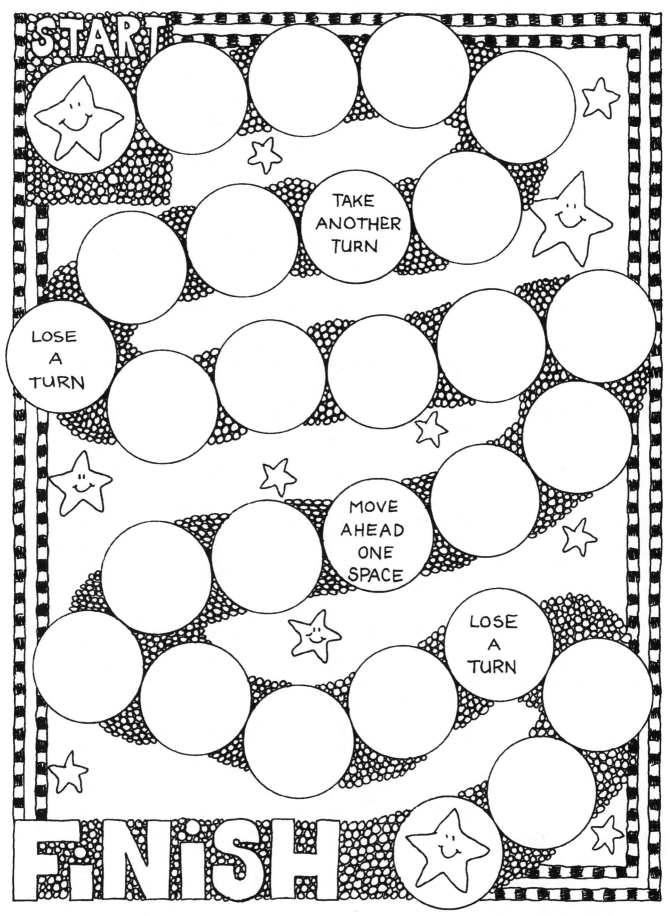

START

TAKE ANOTHER TURN

LOSE A TURN

MOVE AHEAD ONE SPACE

LOSE A TURN

FINISH

29

ESL Reading and Spelling
Games, Puzzles, and Inventive Exercises

Singular vs. Plural Game Cards

Lady	Puppies	Key	Girls
Teachers	Church	Friend	Fish
Foot	Doctor	City	Grass
Beach	Monkey	Umbrella	Mouse
Pencil	Peach	Fox	Countries
Family	Dress	Lunches	Dish
Box	Lollipops	Pennies	Sister
Money	Child	Men	Pony

ESL Reading and Spelling
Games, Puzzles, and Inventive Exercises

Copyright ©2001 by Incentive Publications, Inc.
Nashville, TN.

Encyclopedia Explorers

Purpose:

    Reading - Research

Materials:

    Encyclopedia

    Copy of the research activity

    Pencils

    Colored pencils

Number of Players:

    Four or six

Preparation Directions:

1. Give each player a copy of the research activity.

2. Provide encyclopedia, pencils, and colored pencils.

Player Directions:

1. The players explore the encyclopedias to complete the activity worksheets.

2. When completed, the players share the activity.

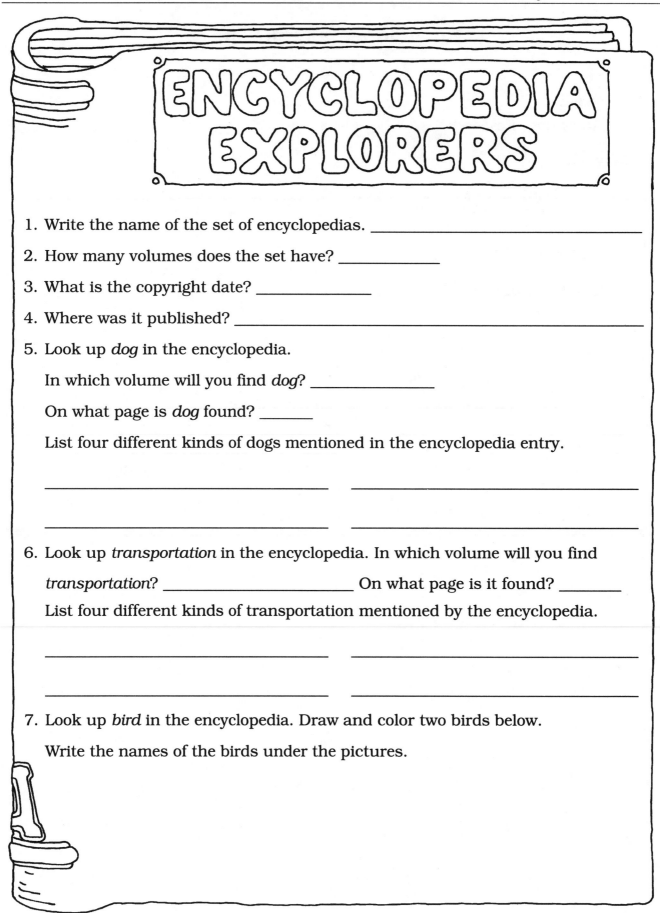

ENCYCLOPEDIA EXPLORERS

1. Write the name of the set of encyclopedias. _____

2. How many volumes does the set have? _____

3. What is the copyright date? _____

4. Where was it published? _____

5. Look up *dog* in the encyclopedia.

   In which volume will you find *dog*? _____

   On what page is *dog* found? _____

   List four different kinds of dogs mentioned in the encyclopedia entry.

   _____   _____

   _____   _____

6. Look up *transportation* in the encyclopedia. In which volume will you find

   transportation? _____ On what page is it found? _____

   List four different kinds of transportation mentioned by the encyclopedia.

   _____   _____

   _____   _____

7. Look up *bird* in the encyclopedia. Draw and color two birds below.

   Write the names of the birds under the pictures.

ENCYCLOPEDIA EXPLORERS

8. Write the name of your native country. _____

   Find this country in the encyclopedia.

   What is the capital? _____

   How many pages are there about your country? _____

   What language is spoken in your country? _____

   Look at the map to find the city in your country where you lived.

   On the back of this activity, draw and color a map of your native country.

9. Look up *flag* in the encyclopedia.

   In what volume will you find *flag*? _____

   Draw your native country's flag here.

10. Choose a topic that you would like to read about in the encyclopedia.

    Write that topic here: _____

    List two things that you learned about this topic.

    1. _____

    _____

    2. _____

    _____

Vowel Volcano

Purpose:

Reading - Long and Short Vowels

Materials:

Copy of game board

Pencils

Number of Players:

Two, or the entire class

Preparation Directions:

1. Give each player a copy of the game.

2. Provide pencils for the students.

Player Directions:

1. The players place the game face down.

2. At a given signal, the players will read the words in the volcano.

3. The players write the words with a short vowel sound and a long vowel sound in the correct spaces.

4. The first player who completes the game wins.

Vowel Volcano Game Board

1. Find the words that have a short vowel sound. Color each one yellow.
2. Find the words that have a long vowel sound. Color each one green.

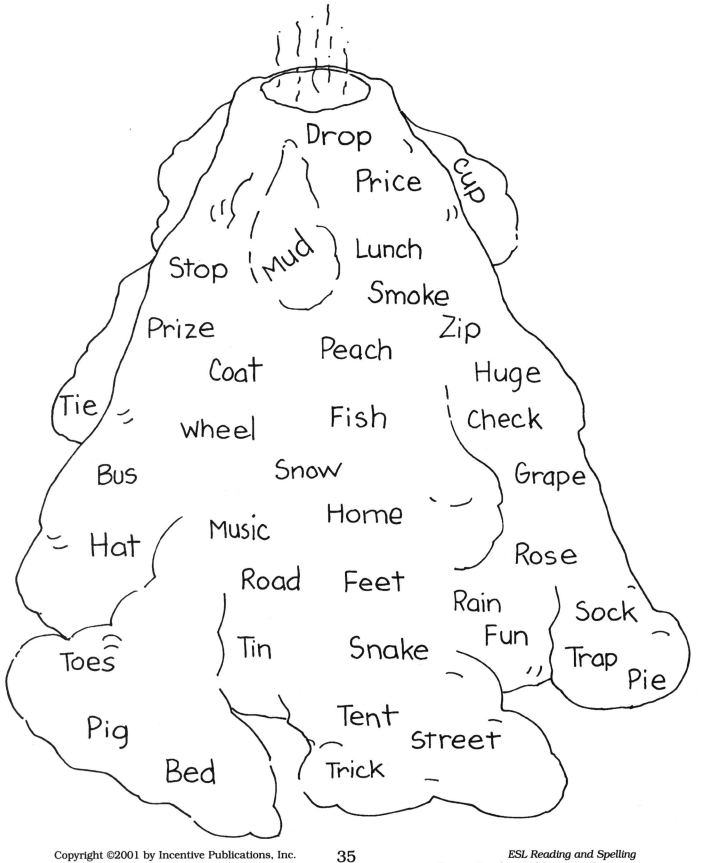

Vowel Volcano

Short Vowel Words	Long Vowel Words
_____	_____
_____	_____
_____	_____
_____	_____
_____	_____
_____	_____
_____	_____
_____	_____
_____	_____
_____	_____
_____	_____
_____	_____
_____	_____
_____	_____
_____	_____
_____	_____
_____	_____

ESL Reading and Spelling
Games, Puzzles, and Inventive Exercises

The Lost Balloon

Purpose:

    Reading - Comprehension, sequence, rhyming words,
        long and short vowels

Materials:

    Copy of the game activities

    Pencils

    Crayons

Number of Players:

    One, two, or the entire class

Preparation Directions:

1. Give each player a copy of the game activities and provide pencils and crayons.

2. Review the following concepts with the students:

    Sequence

    Rhyming Words

    Long and Short Vowels

Player Directions:

1. The players read the story silently first, and then they read it aloud to a partner.

2. To check comprehension, the players answer the questions about the story.

3. The players draw pictures about the story in sequence.

4. Then the players complete the activities with rhyming words and long and short vowels.

The Lost Balloon — A Story

Anna and her family went to the park. Anna played on the swings with some new friends. She fed the ducks. When they were leaving the park, her father bought a big red balloon for her. The wind was blowing very hard, and the balloon went flying up in the sky. Anna was sad and began to cry.

When Anna and her family got home, she saw something on her mailbox. It looked like a big red ball, but it wasn't. It was her red balloon that her father bought for her! Anna ran to get the balloon, but just as she touched the balloon, it popped!

Out fell a note. The note said, "This is a lucky balloon. Whoever finds it can bring this note and get a free balloon every time he or she comes to the park!" Anna was sad to lose her balloon, but she was happy to know she could get another balloon soon.

1. Where did Anna and her family go? _____

2. Write two things Anna did in the park.

   _____

   _____

3. Who bought her a balloon? _____

4. What color was the balloon? _____

5. What happened to the balloon? _____

   _____

6. Where did Anna find the balloon? _____

7. What was inside the balloon? _____

8. What did the note say? _____

   _____

9. Write two feelings that Anna had about the balloon.

   _____

   _____

The Lost Balloon Activity

Draw pictures of Anna that tell the story in sequence. Color the pictures.

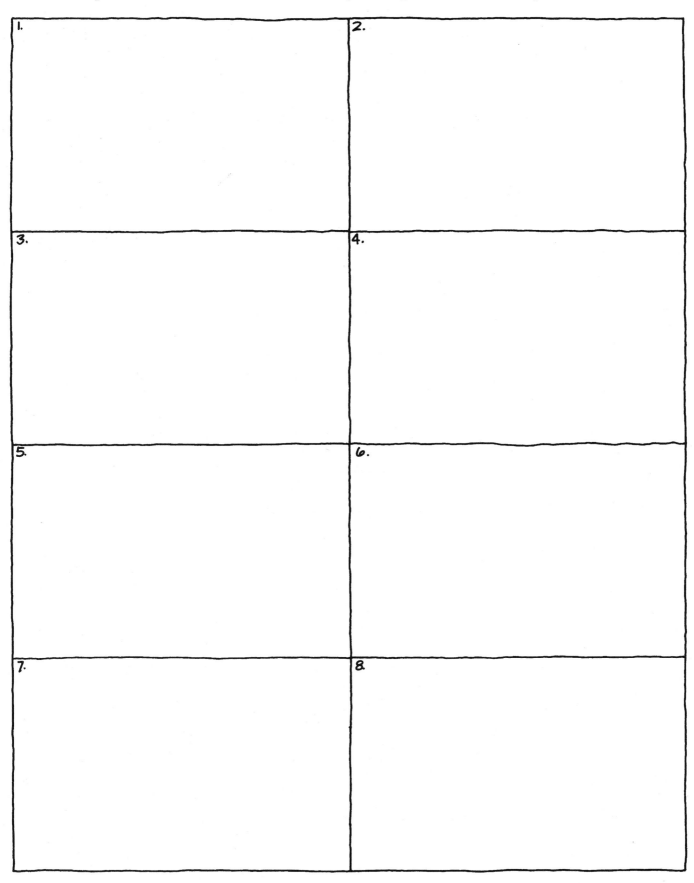

ESL Reading and Spelling
Games, Puzzles, and Inventive Exercises

Write a rhyming word for each of the following words in the story.

park _____

big _____

Red _____

fly _____

sky _____

sad _____

got _____

mail _____

look _____

ball _____

ran _____

took _____

pop _____

note _____

can _____

soon _____

Count the words in the story that have a short vowel sound, and the words that have a long vowel sound.

There are _____ short vowel sound words.

There are _____ long vowel sound words.

40

Blend Bonanza

Purpose:

    Reading - Consonant blends, puzzles

Materials:

    Copy of puzzles

    Pencils

Number of Players:

    One or two

Preparation Directions:

    1. Review consonant blends.

    2. Give each player a copy of one of the puzzles.

Player Directions:

    1. The players circle the words that contain consonant blends in the word search.

    2. Working in pairs or in cooperative learning groups, players use consonant blend words to complete the crossword puzzle.

Play   Truck   Spoon   Spy

Fly   Tray   Quick   Step

Broken   Sky   Fry   Quack

Brook   Glad   Clean   Drink

Train   Please   Prop   Brother

Black   Clap   Slip   Drip

Spring   Cry   Class   Splash

Blast   Plane   Green   Pretty

Blend Bonanza Puzzle #1

Circle the words that have the following consonant blends:

bl, br   fl, fr   qu

cl, cr   gl, gr   sk, sp, spl, spr, st

dr   pl, pr   tr

b l a s t r p l a n e
l s p l a s h c r y m
a d r i p s p r i n g
c l a p b r o t h e r
k q x p r o p d p t e
f u b r o o k g l r e
r a k e k q c l e a n
y c t t e u l a a i d
s k y t n i a d s n r
t r a y s c s t e p i
o f l y p k s p o o n
p l a y y h t r u c k

*ESL Reading and Spelling
Games, Puzzles, and Inventive Exercises*

Blend Bonanza Puzzle #2

Every word in this puzzle begins or ends with a consonant blend.

Across

1. It is fun to __ __ im in a swimming pool.

3. Birds can __ __ y.

4. Do you like to cli __ __ trees?

6. At school, you sit at a de __ __ .

7. A __ __ uck can carry dirt.

9. A __ __ ue is needed to solve a mystery.

10. If someone gets hurt, he or she might __ __ y.

11. Do you like to ice __ __ ate?

12. Fir __ __ grade comes after kindergarten.

13. It is polite to say __ __ ease.

15. A __ __ ain goes on a track.

Down

1. A __ __ ing is fun on the playground.

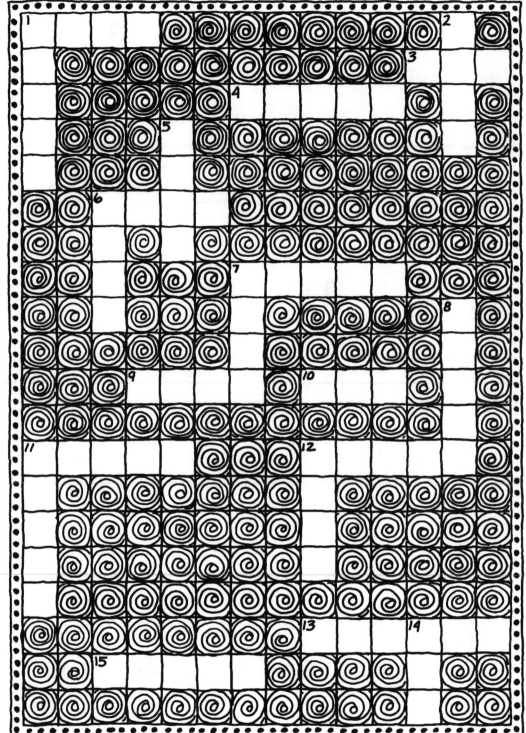

2. __ __ ue is the color of the sky.

5. On Halloween, a ma __ __ is worn.

6. A du __ __ says quack.

7. A __ __ ee grows in a forest.

8. A __ __ ant grows in a garden.

11. __ __ ars are in the sky at night.

12. If you don't have to pay, it is __ __ ee.

14. Students a __ __ questions.

ESL Reading and Spelling Games, Puzzles, and Inventive Exercises

Hidden Pictures

Purpose:

　　Reading - Vocabulary

Materials:

　　Copy of the Hidden Picture game
　　Crayons

Number of Players:

　　One, two, or the entire class

Preparation Directions:

　　1. Give each player a copy of the game and provide crayons.

Player Directions:

　　1. The players find and color the hidden pictures that are shown at the bottom of the page.

　　2. After completing the hidden pictures, the players can color the outdoor scene.

Hidden Pictures Game

 Find the pencil—color it yellow.

 Find the backpack—color it green.

Find the book—color it red.

Find the notebook—color it blue.

 Find the crayons—color them purple.

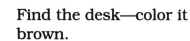 Find the ruler—color it orange.

 Find the erasers—color them pink.

Find the desk—color it brown.

Find the chair—color it black.

Find the computer—color it gray.

Direction Detectives

Purpose:

    Reading - Comprehension, following directions

Materials:

    Copy of activities

    Crayons

    Pencils

Number of Players:

    One, or the entire class

Preparation Directions:

1. Give each student a copy of one of the activities.

2. Provide pencils and crayons.

Player Directions:

1. All of the activities require the students to be able to see and read the directions to complete them.

2. The directions are written on the activities.

Direction Detectives Activity #1

Use your crayons to follow these directions.

1. Put a blue star after anything that is round.
2. Put an orange square after anything that is heavy.
3. Put a red triangle before anything that is light.
4. Put a green circle before anything that is tall.

_____ Snowflake _____   _____ Mountains _____

_____ Potato chip _____   _____ Pencil _____

_____ Tree _____   _____ Raindrop _____

_____ Bracelet _____   _____ Ring _____

_____ Flagpole _____   _____ TV _____

_____ Roller blade wheel _____   _____ Box of books _____

_____ Paper napkin _____   _____ Needle _____

_____ Basketball _____   _____ Bed _____

_____ Apartment building _____   _____ Hamburger _____

_____ Doughnut _____   _____ Piece of paper _____

_____ Car _____   _____ Giant _____

_____ Leaf _____   _____ Orange _____

_____ Penny _____   _____ Paper clip _____

Follow the directions.

1. What flavor would you like this ice cream to be? _____

2. Color it to show the flavor.

3. Draw two ways other than in cones that
   ice cream is sold.

4. This restaurant needs a name.
   Write the name and color the picture of the restaurant.

5. Make a menu for the restaurant.

ESL Reading and Spelling
Games, Puzzles, and Inventive Exercises

1. If a dog likes a cat, write your name under the picture of the snowman.
2. If the bicycle tires are round, draw a circle around the fish.
3. If the fish likes water, color the snowman's hat black.
4. If you can ride a bicycle, draw yourself on the bicycle.
5. If a snowman can melt, draw another snowman beside the picture of the snowman.
6. If you can eat fish, color the fish blue.
7. If a bicycle has brakes, put an X under the picture of the bicycle.
8. If *snowman* is a compound word, draw two snowflakes under this sentence and write one word in each snowflake.

9. If *bicycle* has more than one syllable, write the number of syllables on this line. ____
10. Write the name of each picture in alphabetical order.

_____

_____

_____

The Snowman

Purpose:

Reading - Comprehension, sequence, syllables, writing

Materials:

Copy of game activities

Pencils

Number of Players:

One, two, or the entire class

Preparation Directions:

1. Give each player a copy of the game activities, and provide pencils.

2. Review the concepts of sequence and syllables.

Player Directions:

1. The players read the story, "The Snowman."

2. Divide the class into groups of two. Let students reread the story to each other.

3. The players arrange the sentences in correct order by putting numbers in sequence.

4. The players find words in the story that contain one-, two-, or three-syllable words.

5. To complete the activity, have the students write a story about making a snowman.

The Snowman — A Story

My Lin, Roberto, Teng, and Riham all lived in the same apartment building. One day it snowed, and this was the first time they had ever seen snow. They had seen pictures of a snowman, so they decided to try to make one.

Each one wanted to make part of the snowman. Roberto and Teng would make the largest part. My Lin and Riham would make the middle part, and they would all help make the head and face.

First, Roberto and Teng made a little snowball and began rolling it in the snow until it was a big, big ball. They placed it in a special place. At the same time, My Lin and Riham made a smaller ball of snow. All of the children lifted the smaller ball of snow on top of the larger one that Roberto and Teng had made.

They were now ready to make the head. Carefully, they put the smallest ball of snow on top of the other two. It was beginning to look like a snowman, but it needed a face. The children found some rocks for the eyes and mouth. Two long sticks were used for arms, and a short stick made a good nose. Roberto asked his father to use his hat for the snowman, and My Lin had a pretty red scarf to put around its neck.

When the snowman was all finished, and the children were standing and looking at it, a big van drove up and two men got out. One of the men had a camera and the other had a notebook. They said, "We are from the television station. Can we take your picture and write a story about your snowman?" My Lin, Riham, Roberto, and Teng were so happy that they and their snowman would be on the television news that night.

Write a number beside each sentence to show the sequence of events.

_____ Two men drove up in a van.

_____ The children found some rocks for the eyes and mouth.

_____ It snowed.

_____ Roberto and Teng made the big, big ball.

_____ Sticks were used for the arms and nose.

_____ The children decide to make a snowman.

_____ My Lin puts a red scarf around the snowman's neck.

_____ The smaller snowball was lifted on top of the big ball.

_____ The men took a picture.

_____ Roberto got a hat from his father.

_____ The head was made by all of the children.

_____ My Lin, Roberto, Riham, and Teng will be on the television news.

See how many one-syllable, two-syllable, and three-syllable words you can find in the story.

One-Syllable _____

_____

_____

_____

_____

_____

Two-Syllable _____

_____

_____

_____

_____

_____

Three-Syllable _____

_____

_____

_____

_____

_____

My Snowman

Write a story about a snowman that you have made or that you would like to make.

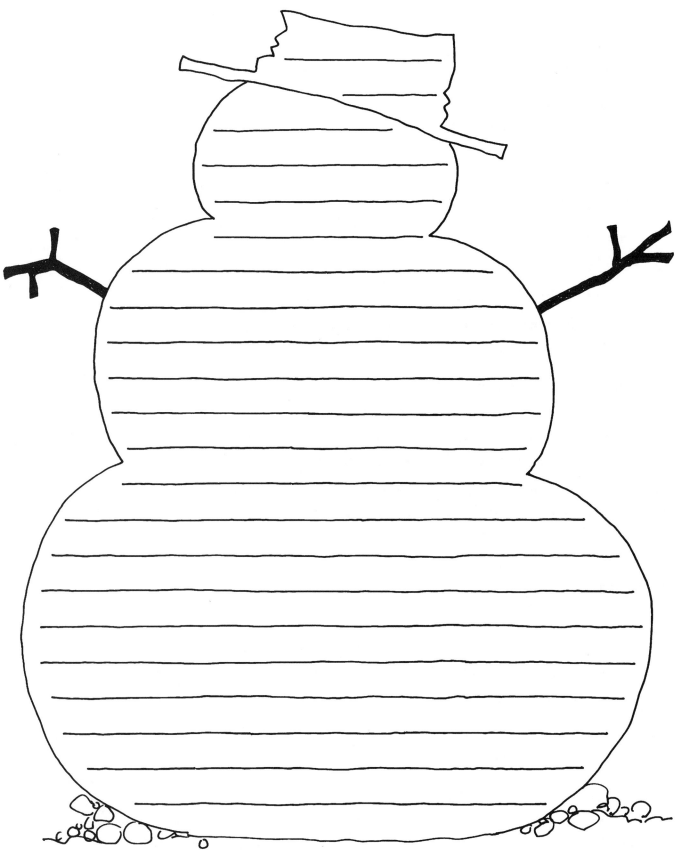

*ESL Reading and Spelling
Games, Puzzles, and Inventive Exercises*

Syllable Spies

Purpose:

    Reading - Syllables

Materials:

    Copy of game

    Pencils

    Crayons

    Kitchen Timer

Number of Players:

    One, two, or the entire class

Preparation Directions:

1. Give each player a copy of the game.
2. Provide pencils and crayons.

Player Directions:

1. The kitchen timer is set for ten minutes.
2. At a given signal, the players write the words, according to the number of syllables, in the correct magnifying glass.
3. The player who completes the game first wins the game.
4. The players can draw and color themselves as a spy on the back of the game.

Zebra	Desk
Boy	Store
Sunshine	Clown
Wonderful	People
Puppy	Butterfly
Circus	Paper
Hospital	Lunch
Shoe	Alligator
Automobile	Sandwich
Flower	Hippopotamus
Cake	Understand
Elephant	Play
Table	Because
Soccer	June
April	Pizza
Ball	Easily
Hamburger	Puzzle
Reading	Cafeteria
Important	Cat
Baseball	Milk
Together	

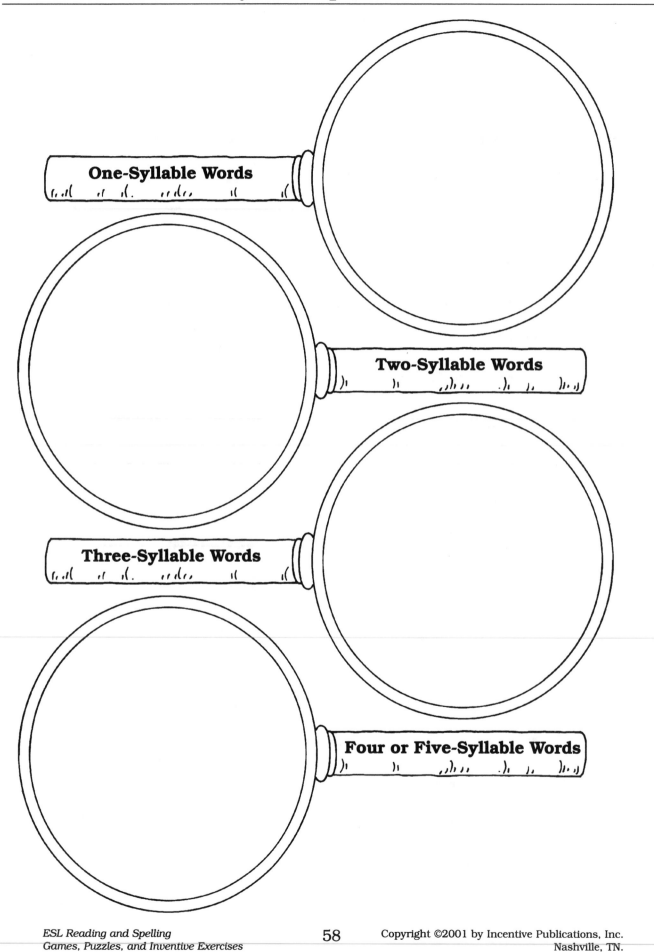

One-Syllable Words

Two-Syllable Words

Three-Syllable Words

Four or Five-Syllable Words

Secret Code

Purpose:

    Reading - Alphabetical Order

Materials:

    Copy of game sheet

    Pencils

    Answers to Secret Code Game Sheet:

    1. What is your name?

    2. How old are you?

    3. In what city do you live?

    4. Where do you go to school?

    5. What language do you speak?

    6. In what country did you live?

    7. What is your address?

    8. What time is it now?

Number of Players:

    Two

Preparation Directions:

    1. Give each player a copy of the game sheet.

    2. Provide pencils.

Player Directions:

    1. The players have a copy of the game.

    2. To understand the code, the players must write the letter that comes before the letter that is written in code.
       Example: 'n' becomes 'm'
                  'b' becomes 'a'
                  'o' becomes 'n' (spelling "man")

    3. On the back of the game, students can write a secret message using the same code.

Secret Code Game Board

1. xibu jt zpvs obnf?

   _ _ _ _ _ _ _ _ _ _ _ _ _ _ _ ?

2. Ipx pme bsf zpv?

   _ _ _ _ _ _ _ _ _ _ _ _ ?

3. Jo xibu djuz ep zpv mjwf?

   _ _ _ _ _ _ _ _ _ _ _ _ _ _ _ _ _ _ _ _ ?

4. Xifsf ep zpv hp up tdippm?

   _ _ _ _ _ _ _ _ _ _ _ _ _ _ _ _ _ _ _ _ ?

5. Xibu mbohvbhf ep zpu tqfbl?

   _ _ _ _ _ _ _ _ _ _ _ _ _ _ _ _ _ _ _ _ _ _ ?

6. Jo xibu dpvousz eje zpv mjwf?

   _ _ _ _ _ _ _ _ _ _ _ _ _ _ _ _ _ _ _ _ _ _ _ ?

7. Xibu jt zpvs beesftt?

   _ _ _ _ _ _ _ _ _ _ _ _ _ _ _ _ _ ?

8. Xibu ujnf jt ju opx?

   _ _ _ _ _ _ _ _ _ _ _ _ _ _ _ ?

Tic Tac Toe

Purpose:

Spelling

Materials:

Tag board

Black markers

Number of Players:

Two

Preparation Directions:

1. Use tag board and black marker to make five tag board O's and five tag board X's.

2. Prepare tag board strips with the weekly spelling words written on them.

Player Directions:

1. Players place the spelling cards face down and choose markers.

2. The first player draws a card and pronounces the spelling word. If his or her opponent spells the word correctly, he or she places the marker on the board.

3. The game continues until one player gets a tic tac toe horizontally, vertically, or diagonally.

Tic Tac Toe Game Board

ESL Reading and Spelling
Games, Puzzles, and Inventive Exercises

Blast Off

Purpose:

Spelling

Materials:

Tag board

Black marker

Number of Players:

Two

Preparation Directions:

1. Make a rocket out of tag board. (Draw two sets of twelve lines on the rocket.)

2. Write spelling words in pieces of tag board the same width as the lines on the rocket.

Player Directions:

1. Shuffle the spelling word cards. Place the cards on the rocket.

2. One player draws a card and pronounces the word for the other player to spell.

3. If the word is spelled correctly, the player places the card on the rocket beside the number ten.

4. The game continues until one player reaches zero and "Blast off!"

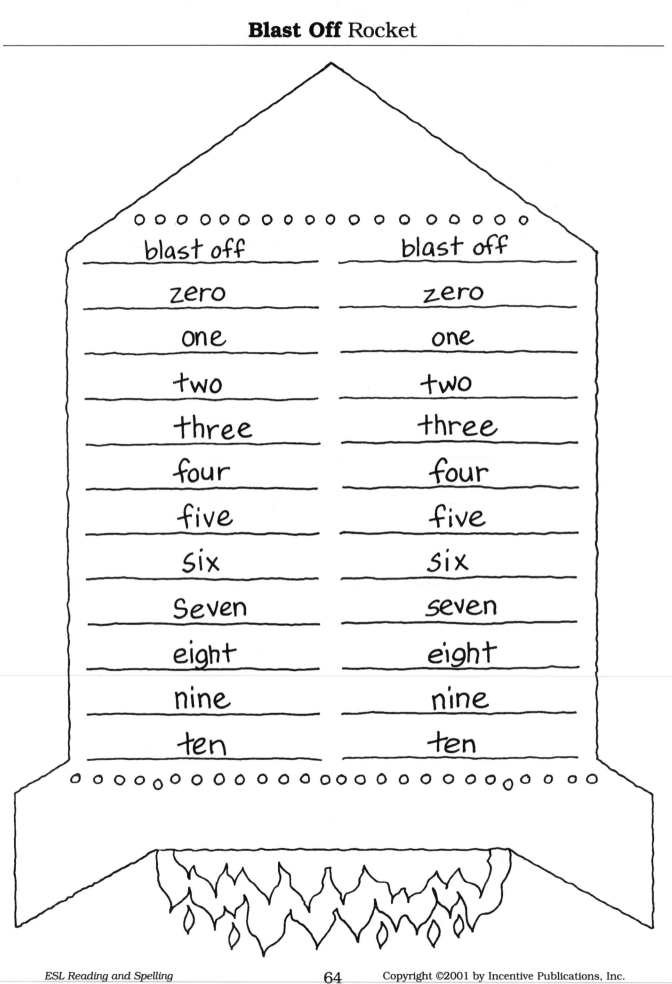

Spelling Checkers

Purpose:

Spelling

Materials:

Checkerboard on page 66

Tag board in two different colors

Black marker

Number of Players:

Two

Preparation Directions:

1. Make 24 checkers from two colors of tag board, so that there are 12 checkers of each color.

2. On the back of each checker write a spelling word from the weekly list.

3. Extra checkers can be made to provide different spelling words each time the game is played.

Player Directions:

1. Two players place checkers on board.

2. One player moves a checker. If he can jump his opponent's checker, the opponent looks under the checker to be jumped and pronounces the word.

3. If the player can spell the word correctly, he may jump and pick up the checker.

4. The game continues until one player is out of checkers and is declared "the winner."

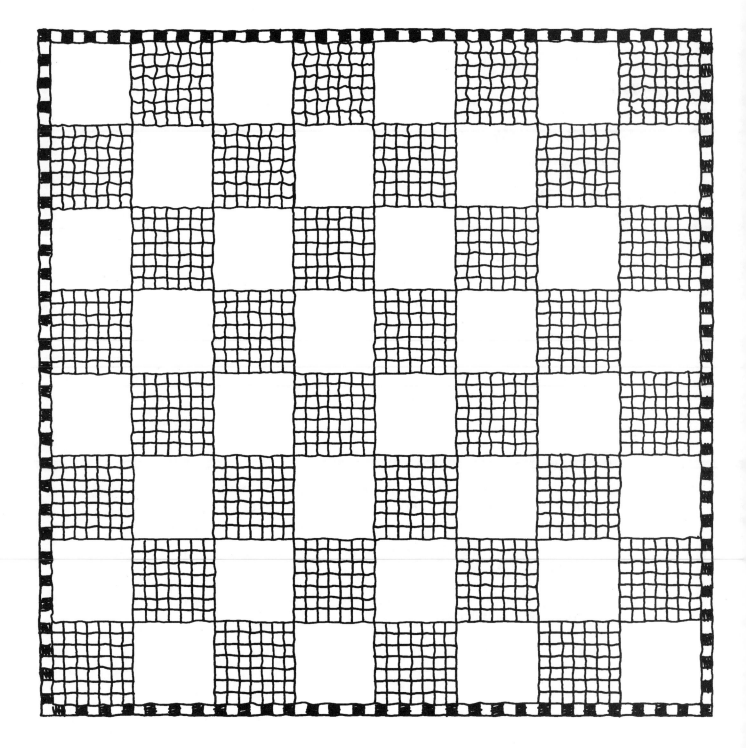

Drive and Spell

Purpose:

Spelling

Materials:

Tag board

Toy cars

Markers

Number of Players:

Two or three

Preparation Directions:

1. Enlarge the playing board on page 68 on tag board to be used as a game board.

2. Provide small toy cars or draw and cut out tag board paper cars for each player.

3. Write each spelling word on a tag board card; place a star on the most difficult words.

Player Directions:

1. Choose a car and place it on the board.

2. One player draws a card and reads the word aloud to the other player.

3. He then spells the word. If he spells it correctly, he moves ahead one space. If he spells it incorrectly, he moves back one space. When a starred word is spelled, the player moves ahead two spaces.

4. The first player to reach home wins the game.

Drive and Spell Game Board

*ESL Reading and Spelling
Games, Puzzles, and Inventive Exercises*

Copyright ©2001 by Incentive Publications, Inc.
Nashville, TN.

Correct Colors

Purpose:

Spelling - Colors

Materials:

Copy of game activities

Crayons

Scissors

Paste

Pencils

Number of Players:

Two

Preparation Directions:

1. Give each player a copy of the game activities.

2. Provide crayons, scissors, paste, and pencils for the students.

Player Directions:

1. The players cut out the crayon shapes and place them face down.

2. The first player draws a crayon shape and asks the other player to spell the color that is written on it.

3. If the player spells the color word correctly, the first player gives the color shape to him or her.

4. Taking turns, the game continues until all of the color words have been spelled correctly.

5. The players color the crayon shapes.

6. Next, the players paste the crayon shapes on the crayon box shape activity. The players may color the crayon box shape.

7. On the last activity, the players draw two things that could be the color which is written on each box.

8. The players color the pictures.

*ESL Reading and Spelling
Games, Puzzles, and Inventive Exercises*

Correct Colors Crayons

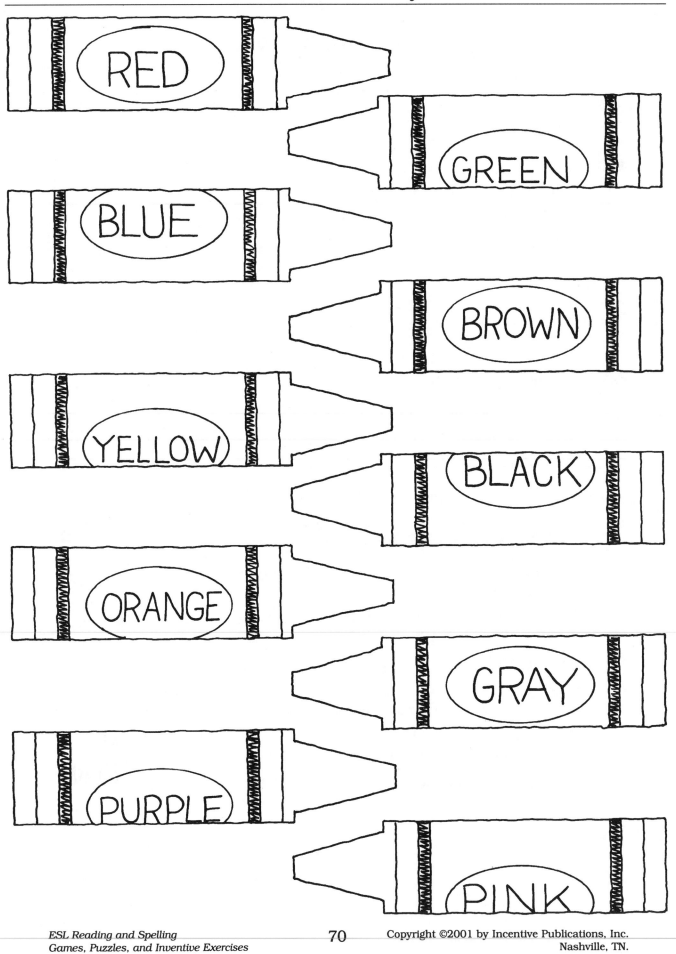

Cut on dotted lines
and slip in crayons.

ESL Reading and Spelling
Games, Puzzles, and Inventive Exercises

Correct Colors Activity Sheet

Draw a picture of something that is the same color that is written in each box below. Color the pictures.

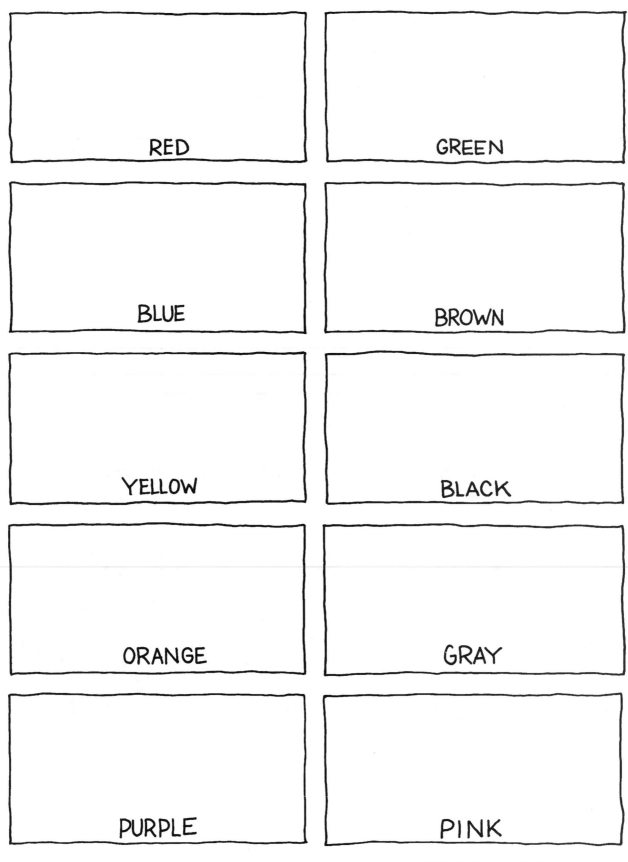

RED

GREEN

BLUE

BROWN

YELLOW

BLACK

ORANGE

GRAY

PURPLE

PINK

ESL Reading and Spelling
Games, Puzzles, and Inventive Exercises

Play Ball

Purpose:

Spelling

Materials:

Poster board

Felt tip pens

Scissors

Game markers

Number of Players:

Two

Preparation Directions:

1. Make a baseball diamond out of poster board: include all the bases. Make markers in the shape of a baseball bat and a ball.

2. Write spelling words on poster board strips labeled according to level of difficulty. The least difficult words will be labeled as "single hits," next level as "doubles," next level "triples," and the most difficult level as "home runs."

Player Directions:

1. The cards are placed face down and each player chooses a marker.

2. The first player "goes to bat" by choosing a card without looking at it. The second player "pitches" the word on the card by pronouncing the word for the "batter" to spell. The player who is at bat may choose a spelling word from any stack. Example: If a word from "doubles" is chosen and spelled correctly, the batter goes to second base. One point is awarded each time a player in the "batter" position passes home plate. If a word is misspelled, it is an out. Three outs and the pitcher is allowed to become the batter. If the batter spells the word correctly, he or she continues to spell words drawn from the stack and pronounced by the player "pitching" words until three words are misspelled.

3. The game continues until nine innings have been played. One inning is complete when both players have had a chance to "bat." The player with the most points wins the game.

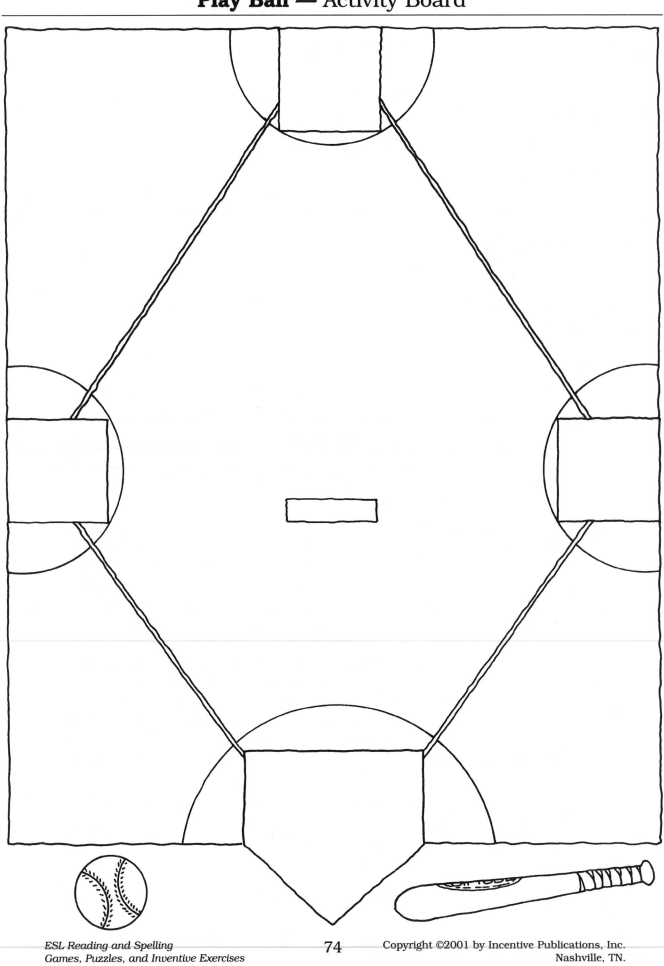

*ESL Reading and Spelling
Games, Puzzles, and Inventive Exercises*

74

Annotated Bibliography
for the ESL Teacher

BASIC/Not Boring Reading Comprehension, Grades 4-5. Imogene Forte and Marjorie Frank. Nashville, Incentive Publications, Inc., 1998
Imaginative activities covering essential reading skills such as: main ideas, finding information, sequencing, and paraphrasing.

BASIC/Not Boring Spelling, Grades 4-5, Imogene Forte and Marjorie Frank. Nashville, Incentive Publications, Inc., 1999
Imaginative activities covering essential spelling skills such as: identifying correctly spelled and misspelled words, learning the "ie" rules, and distinguishing among homophones.

BASIC/Not Boring Reading, Grades 2-3. Imogene Forte and Marjorie Frank. Nashville, Incentive Publications, Inc., 1998
Imaginative activities covering essential reading skills such as: main idea, sequencing, charts, directions, and characters.

BASIC/Not Boring Spelling, Grades 2-3. Imogene Forte and Marjorie Frank. Nashville, Incentive Publications, Inc. 2000
Imaginative activities covering essential spelling skills such as: compound words, consonant blends, and frequently misspelled words.

The Cooperative Learning Guide and Planning Pak for the Primary Grades. Imogene Forte and Joy MacKenzie. Nashville, Incentive Publications, Inc., 1992
Includes an overview of cooperative learning and thematic teaching, content mini-units, interdisciplinary units, and thematic learning stations.

Cooperative Learning Teacher Timesavers. Imogene Forte. Nashville, Incentive Publications, Inc., 1992
Contains summaries, warm-ups, bulletin boards, and cooperative activities, and motivational ideas, as well as ready-to-use reproducible aids, badges, clip art, reports, worksheets, and records.

Creating Connection: Learning to Appreciate Diversity. Dorothy Michener. Nashville, Incentive Publications, Inc., 1995
Provides practical strategies and workable solutions for educators striving to help their students recognize, understand, and appreciate diversity.

Easy Art Projects to Teach Global Awareness. Lynn Brisson. Nashville, Incentive Publications, Inc., 1993
Topics covered include map skills, the 50 United States, the 7 continents, desert and ocean study, and more!

ESL Active Learning Lessons: 15 Complete Content-Based Units to Reinforce Language Skills and Concepts. Imogene Forte and Mary Ann Pangle. Nashville, Incentive Publications, Inc., 2001
Provides practice and reinforcement in the use of listening, speaking, reading and writing.

ESL Content-Based Language Games, Puzzles, and Inventive Exercises. Imogene Forte and
Mary Ann Pangle. Nashville, Incentive Publications, Inc., 2001
Offers useable guides to learn, practice, and master a variety of language-based skills,
focusing on math, social studies, and science.

ESL Vocabulary and Word Usage Games, Puzzles, and Inventive Exercises. Imogene Forte and
Mary Ann Pangle. Nashville, Incentive Publications, Inc., 2001
Offers useable guides to learn, practice, and master a variety of language-based skills,
focusing on vocabulary and word usage.

Hands-On Math. Kathleen Fletcher. Nashville, Incentive Publications, Inc., 1996
Contains all the essentials and extras for teaching number-sense concepts. Included
ideas for using stamps, stickers, beans, rice, tiles, and number lines and manipulatives in
the classroom.

Internet Quest. Catherine Halloran Cook and Janet McGivney Pfeifer. Nashville, Incentive
Publications, Inc., 2000
Designed to engage students in learning on the web. 101 new sites to explore covering
exciting topics such as: art and music, geography and travel, nature and science.

Language Arts Folder Fun. Kathy Blankenhorn and Joanne Richards. Nashville, Incentive
Publications, Inc., 1995
Folder games target and reinforce the fundamentals of language arts.

Learning to Learn: Strengthening Study Skills and Brain Power. Gloria Frender. Nashville,
Incentive Publications, Inc., 1990
Includes step-by-step procedures for improving organizational skills, time management,
problem solving, power reading, test taking, memory skills, and more!

Multicultural Plays: A Many-Splendored Tapestry Honoring Our Global Community. Judy Mecca.
Nashville, Incentive Publications, Inc., 1999
Easily-produced plays allow students to learn about and develop respect for different
cultures. A brief cultural lesson accompanies each play to ensure an authentic performance.

On the Loose With Dr. Seuss. Shirley Cook. Nashville, Incentive Publications, Inc., 1994
Each literature-based unit includes background information about Dr. Seuss and one of
his stories, extended thinking and writing exercises, and special imaginative activities.

Reading Reinforcers for the Primary Grades. Imogene Forte. Nashville, Incentive Publications,
Inc., 1994
A collection of teacher-directed interactive projects, creative worksheets, and independent
and group activities.

Seasonal Activities for Classroom Creativity. Kitty Hazler. Nashville, Incentive
Publications, Inc., 1999
High-interest lessons to nurture creativity and promote higher order thinking skills within
a seasonal theme. Students gain fluency and originality.

Using Literature to Learn About Children Around the World. Judith Cochran. Nashville,
Incentive Publications, Inc., 1993
Lesson plans outline specific activities to develop social and global awareness and to
strengthen vocabulary and thinking skills.

Answer Key

Pages 24-25
1. table   7. duck
2. bed   8. flower
3. tv   9. pizza
4. bike   10. cat
5. school   11. star
6. pencil   12. clock

Page 27
Across

1. Mon   19. oct
4. st   21. pres
5. oz   24. sp
7. min   25. sun
9. TN   29. Apr
10. pm   30. MD
13. Rev   31. wed
14. dr   33. mar
16. dz

Down

1. Mr   18. ml
2. Nov   20. Tues
3. RR   21. pt
4. Sat   22. Sr
6. VP   23. N
7. Math   26. Thurs
8. no   27. Jan
11. Aug   28. Feb
12. Rd   30. Mrs
15. Sept   32. ft
17. ok   33. mi

Page 30
lady - ladies
puppies - puppy
key - keys
girls - girl
teachers - teacher
church - churches
friend - friends
fish - fishes
foot - feet
doctor - doctors
city - cities
grass - grasses
beach - beaches
monkey - monkeys
umbrella - umbrellas
mouse - mice
pencil - pencils

peach - peaches
countries - country
fox - foxes
family - families
dress -dresses
lunches - lunch
dish - dishes
box - boxes
lollipops - lollipop
pennies - penny
sister - sisters
money - monies
child - children
men - man
pony - ponies

Page 35
Words with short vowel sounds colored yellow:

Hat	Fun	Drop
Tin	Sock	Tent
Mud	Bed	Trap
Cup	Pig	Hug
Stop	Fish	Bus
Trick	Zip	Lunch
	Check	

Words with long vowel sounds colored green:

Snake	Rain	Grape
Music	Rose	Coat
Road	Toes	Smoke
Feet	Pie	Tie
Home	Wheel	Price
Street	Snow	Prize
	Peach	

Page 38
1. the park
2. She played on the swings, she fed the ducks, and her father bought her a red balloon.
3. her father
4. red
5. The wind blew it away.
6. on the mailbox at her house
7. a note
8. "This is a lucky balloon. Whoever finds it can bring this note and get a free balloon every time you come to the park!"
9. sad and happy

Page 43

Page 44

△ Snowflake _____   ○ Mountains ▢
△★ Potato chip _____   △ Pencil _____
○ Tree ▢   ★ Raindrop _____
★ Bracelet _____   ★ Ring _____
○ Flagpole ▢   _____ TV ▢
★ Roller blade wheel _____   _____ Box of books ▢
△ Paper napkin _____   △ Needle _____
★ Basketball _____   _____ Bed ▢
○ Apartment building ▢   ★ Hamburger _____
★ Doughnut _____   △ Piece of paper _____
○ Car ▢   ○ Giant ▢
△ Leaf _____   ★ Orange _____
△★ Penny _____   △ Paper clip _____

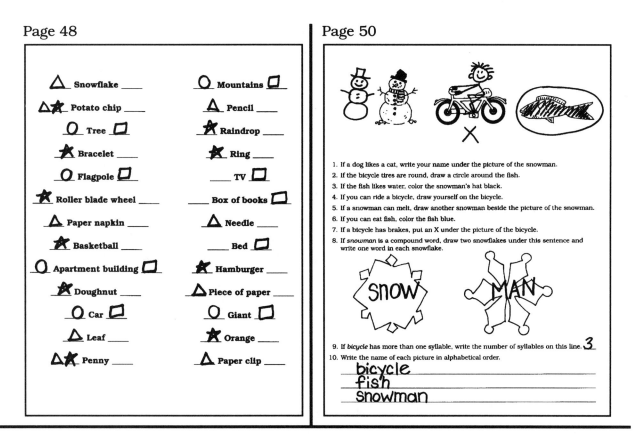

1. If a dog likes a cat, write your name under the picture of the snowman.
2. If the bicycle tires are round, draw a circle around the fish.
3. If the fish likes water, color the snowman's hat black.
4. If you can ride a bicycle, draw yourself on the bicycle.
5. If a snowman can melt, draw another snowman beside the picture of the snowman.
6. If you can eat fish, color the fish blue.
7. If a bicycle has brakes, put an X under the picture of the bicycle.
8. If *snowman* is a compound word, draw two snowflakes under this sentence and write one word in each snowflake.

snow   MAN

9. If *bicycle* has more than one syllable, write the number of syllables on this line. 3
10. Write the name of each picture in alphabetical order.
   bicycle _____
   fish _____
   snowman _____

Page 53

The proper sequence is as follows: 10, 6, 1, 3, 7, 2, 9, 4, 11, 8, 5, 12

Page 58

One-syllable words:	Two-syllable words:	Three-syllable words:
Boy	Zebra	Wonderful
Shoe	Sunshine	Hospital
Cake	Puppy	Elephant
Ball	Circus	Hamburger
Desk	Flower	Important
Store	Table	Together
Clown	Soccer	Butterfly
Lunch	April	Understand
Play	Reading	Easily
June	Baseball	
Cat	People	Four- and five-syllable words:
Milk	Paper	Automobile
	Sandwich	Alligator
	Because	Hippopotamus
	Pizza	Cafeteria
	Puzzle	

Page 60

1. What is your name?
2. How old are you?
3. In what city do you live?
4. Where do you go to school?
5. What language do you speak?
6. In what country did you live?
7. What is your address?
8. What time is it now?